MY TESTIMONY

That Voice Within Me

BY
MALCOLM AJ CHARLES

 www.trafford.com

North America & international
toll-free: 1 888 232 4444 (USA & Canada)
phone: 250 383 6864 ♦ fax: 812 355 4082

CONTENTS

FOREWORD

"I came that you may have life and have it more abundantly". (John 10; V10).

It was the Rev Dr. Winston Worrel, Director of the World Evangelism Methodist Institute who had been encouraging us in the Caribbean, to "indigenize the Gospel", by using everyday aspects of our lives and culture, to communicate what God has done and can do for us.

When God spoke to the Israelites as he led them out of Egypt, he spoke to them in their own language and culture.

It is therefore in our work, our family, our music, our dance, our worship, that God speaks to us today.

He speaks to us in our language, but the message never changes!!

God wants to bring you to your "potential heights" as what was meant for your harm, he will turn it around and use it for your good.

I am therefore pleased to have been invited by Bro Malcolm Charles, to present the Foreword of his Book of Testimony, where the Lord has intervened positively in his life and for his courage to share those experiences in writing, to encourage others to keep the faith.

May God bless you all.

Rev Madet Merove
Superintendent Minister
The Methodist Church
Saint Lucia Circuit

CHAPTER ONE (1)

Overcoming Asthma Attacks

Having arrived on this fair earth via a premature birth, as a child, all wrapped up in cotton wool as a make shift incubator I am told, I thereafter suffered immensely with Asthma attacks, causing me to miss school lessons and as a result, I had to "struggle" through classes at both the Primary through to mid Secondary School levels.

My parents and family members prayed and prayed for my relief from this affliction, while at the same time, consulting with our caring and empathetic family physicians, in the persons of the late Dr. Sir Frederick Clarke and Dr. Betty Wells.

It was not until age 15, when the prognosis of the late Dr.Betty Wells came to past, that the asthma 'curse' was finally lifted from me, and by God's grace, I outgrew the condition to this day.

While I may not have fully understood it back then, now in my more mature years, it is clear, that the good Lord had in fact intervened and has thankfully, continued to the present time.

As it is written in Psalms 103, "Bless the Lord, O my soul, and forget not all his benefits; who forgiveth all thine iniquities; who healeth all thy diseases"

All Praise and thanks therefore, be to Almighty God.

Parents Wedding Photo
1947

CHAPTER TWO (2)

"You Must Behave For An Hour"

The title of this Testimony, was the regular and consistent "chant" of my late father Percy, both at home and at Sunday school in particular, as he exhorted the "restless youth of the day" attending the Methodist Sunday School, of which he was Superintendent.

The rationale of "You must behave for an hour", was that if you could be disciplined enough to behave yourself during the "one hour" duration of Sunday School sessions, then your chances of becoming "self disciplined", could be incrementally improved.

According to Dad's logic, and I quote "If you can be successful at behaving for an hour (at Sunday school) then you could try two hours, then three hours, six, eight hours, a day, a week, a month, a year, until your entire life becomes one of self discipline."

You know I will have to admit that our "patriarch" I believe was right!!

Even as I travelled various countries around the world, I would from time to time run into some of my former 'Sunday School Classmates' who continue (even to this day) to quote those recurring lines 'You must behave for an hour', as well as in my own life, notwithstanding difficult and trying times, these words are again Testimony to God's Grace.

Even today, I call on that inner strength, to "tide" me through, when things go contrary to what I expect.

Like the old "count to ten" formula, I simply try to "cope for an hour" then onwards incrementally . . . .

I recommend that you try it when next you are confronted with another 'patience testing' dilemma.

All Praise and Glory be to the most high . . . .

CHAPTER THREE (3)

GeestLine Ship-With whom I once worked
(60's to 90's)

"Move Now"—
(That Mysterious Voice)

T he "Bay Street" Docks at the Waterfront of Kingstown St.Vincent back in 1971, was the scene of a near mishap, that I will never ever be able to forget . . .

As a young man, having performed my duties at the Company's Saint Lucia based regional Head Quarters and dockside operations, in keeping with the apparent expectations of the days directorate, I had the privilege of being accorded the designation of the Company's First (West Indian) "Management Trainee" in the Windward Islands, and effective January 1971, was to "hold myself in readiness for inter company attachments and transfers."

St.Vincent was therefore in effect, my first "overseas attachment", which I accepted with great enthusiasm, determined to deliver the best I could, to justify that apparent "confidence" placed in me, by my Directors of the day.

I took up residence at a nearby "Bay Street" Apartment Building known as "The Heron Hotel", which was located right across the street from the Kingstown Harbour opposite the main entrance to the Geest Shipping compound, through which St.Vincent conducted its Fruit and Produce Exports, while reciprocally receiving manufactured imports from overseas.

The Supervision of weekly Exports and Imports on the dockside and the accompanying 'admin' work in the office, became part of my regular work routine, alongside my team of "Vincy" colleagues.

One day, whilst at work down in the 'D' deck of the ship's hold (4 floors down) my shipping colleague and I were supervising the unloading of general cargo from the early hours of the morning, in preparation for receiving Banana Exports aboard ship later that day.

Cranes 'screamed' under the strain of their loads, superseded only by the din of shouts and orders coming to and from the stevedores themselves.

"Whoa, heads up, untie the slings, tie, pull, lift, Watch yourself man', were among the "shouts" exchanged by the 'gang' assigned to the discharge of the particular cargo hatch.

In the midst of all of the 'halabalou', all of a sudden, the noise around me appeared to die down, and a strange but somehow displaced 'silence' seemed to prevail, notwithstanding that the work at hand, still continued at a pace.

Then came a calm, but decisive voice in my head, "Move Now" the voice beckoned, "Move Nowww" . . . . !

Wondering where that voice came from, I grabbed my adjacent colleague by the upper arm and pulled him about fifteen (15) feet, back under the hatch coaming.

As he looked at me to ask shockingly, "What are you doing?" (He never finished the sentence) only managing to say "Wh . . . ." there was a loud crashing noise, coming from right where we had been standing.

We turned around to see, a forklift truck disintegrating (almost in 'slow motion') with engine oil spilling one way, the battery another way and parts of the unit splattered all over the deck.

Perhaps owing to sea swells in the Kingstown Harbour that day, the forklift truck had simply slid off the 'A' Deck where it was parked and fell four floors onto the aluminum deck where we had been standing, just seconds ago!.

The large cavity in the aluminum deck floor left by the impact, drove "shudders" through my spine, as I realized what had just happened.

It was evident that had we remained in the particular spot where we had been standing, we both would have been crushed beyond recognition.!!

Our names with time, would have been mere 'statistics' of the past having been pasted perhaps, in the 'Vincy' obituaries . . . today, a vague recollection of our existence.

As a young man, of twenty years in age at best, I struggled with the 'mystery' of the voice, that drove me to "Move Now" . . . for years on end.

Whose "voice" was it, I would ask myself, especially when I lay exhausted in bed at my Bay Street apartment.

Afraid perhaps of being "ridiculed" by colleagues and friends that it was "God's

Voice", I kept the 'story' to myself, possibly for the next decade at least, lest I was considered as being eligible for registration at the nearest "Mental Asylum" as the "Trainee who God spoke to".!

As years rolled by, there were similar (albeit less dramatic) experiences, all of which I could in no way attribute to mere coincidence, nor were they incidents, outcomes or happy endings, I might have attributed to my own making.

No my brothers and sisters, it is today indelibly etched in my mind and heart, that all along it was "The Voice of God" which had intervened and shielded me from the potential peril that had encircled me on that day, which without doubt, would have been my last.

I therefore unhesitatingly give thanks and praise to Almighty God for his intervention on that almost fateful day and the many interventions that have followed since.

I stand in readiness and await his direction, on what he has in store for me in his earthly vineyard, to offer up to him in return.

Meanwhile, I will continue to do what I consider my best, by helping others in his honour.

All praise and thanks to the most High God for directing my steps into the future . . . .

CHAPTER FOUR (4)

The "Power Of
Bold Faith"

I recall tuning into to one of my favorite 'televangelists' sometime ago, and he was challenging his congregation to pray what he called "Bold Prayers", as he illustrated a Bible text that, our "receiving" will in proportion to ability to "open our mouths wide."

Don't just ask God for "Barely enough" to get by, he said, but rather pray for "more than enough", so that you could even be a blessing to others.

This took me back over forty years when I was attending one of my first job interviews, at the age of 19 years, when my potential

Employer leaned over and said to me, "Where exactly do you propose to fit into this organisation?"

I looked him straight in the eye (as best I could) and said "Sir, ideally, I would like to be sitting where you are sitting."

He stuttered with amazement, as this was some 10 years before Saint Lucia's Independence in the colony where we were mere 'subjects' back then(not Citizens), it was not "the sort of thing" a fresh out of high school lad, would say to the so called "big white chief."!!

For my 'fastness', I was none the less offered a job as a 'Statistics Clerk,' which was as boring as jobs could get, designed to frustrate the life out of you(or so it seemed), long before the advent of automated office systems, computers and what have you.

It was clear in succeeding years, that the boss didn't particularly like me, and I suspect, that apart from being the "wrong colour", he would be looking over his shoulder, at what he may have considered, to be "an over ambitious local upstart"!

I took the "boring" statistics job, entering weekly export tonnages and turned it into a "work of art", with statistical charts and graphs in an array of colors and permutations (in a pre computer era mind you), until one day, the Board was to have a meeting with the 'World Chairman', who was in town and they wanted some comparative tonnages, spanning the entire history of the Industry in five year intervals, or some such configuration.

My own boss came to my little desk under the office clock and asked me how long it would take me to compile the data in the format they were looking for . . . .

Reaching down, I pulled out the bottom drawer of my little desk and showed him one of the charts I had earlier prepared, and asked "Would you want something looking like this?"

He scanned it from top to bottom with his glasses perched at the tip of his nose.

"Who asked you to do this?" he said. "No one sir," I replied.

"This is exactly what we want" and took off in haste in the direction of the Board Room.

Moments later, I saw faces of the other board members peering out the board room door in my direction, leaving my 19 year old head, wondering exactly what was going on behind those closed doors.

You know the following January, I received a letter from the then Corporate Secretary, saying that I was appointed the company's first(ever) West Indies "Trainee Manager"?

I took it (the letter) home and showed it to my Dad, who immediately extended his tight grip of a congratulatory handshake, a thank you prayer, followed by a generous 'award' of an "Oh Henry" chocolate followed even further by a glass of 'red wine' which he used for "toasting", anytime there was a breakthrough for any member of the family.

You know for the next 10 years, I was sent on attachments to the various islands where the Business operated at the time, and at same time, had personally taken the initiative, to start a Business Management and Administration Qualification via Distance Education.

On completion of the Foundation stage of the Course programme, I then applied to go to a UK College for another couple years to finish the remaining subjects required to graduate at professional level.

By then, the 'chief', yes my former boss was due for retirement and guess who was asked to 'sit where he was sitting' when I returned home?

He had by then retired and was returning to his homeland overseas . . . I went to see him off and it was an emotional moment when he said to me 'you have stayed the course and I cant think of anyone better' for that role.

The rest as we say is history . . . . I was now 'sitting where he was sitting'.

Without doubt, I recognize the power of "Bold Faith", ten years on from my first job interview with him . . .

CHAPTER FIVE (5)

Self Tuition—Distance Ed

"For unto him that hath, more shall be added, but unto him that hath not, even that which he hath, shall be taken away" Matthew Ch25; v24.

This passage of scripture literally scared the 'living daylights' out of me during the initial stages of my career.

Now back tracking a bit, apart from pressure from my father, to (as he used to put it) 'get your letters,' this proclamation from the Almighty further compounded the need to get quickly onto the 'tertiary qualifications band wagon,' if I was to avert "even that which he hath shall be taken away."

As alluded to earlier, my research into a suitable field of endeavour had begun with an analysis of the subject content of various professional bodies, which upon ultimate student registration, would be complemented by the need to access Distance Education Studies.

Having decided that 'business' was going to take centre stage in my career, I needed to decide whether I wanted to become a Professional in Sales, Marketing, Purchasing & Supply, Export Management, Insurance, Journalism, Maritime Law, Business Management, Administration, Company Secretaryship, Ship Broking, what have you, and the list of options on offer, just seemed endless.

Clearly by earlier process of elimination, it was certainly not going to be (based on subjects acquired and natural instincts so far manifested) any branch of Medicine (not for a guy who historically "passes out" at sight of blood).

Construction and Engineering (not with a fear of heights), Airline Pilots (same thing), Sea Captain (I don't swim), Clergy (well . . .)!!

So after all was said and done and 'ushered' by my mentors of the day, it was all short listed down to "Business Administration & Management, with majors in Human Resources, Marketing and Export Studies.

Again, we are talking here of the colonial, (pre google) days, which meant writing off to the targeted Professional Institute(s) (based either in the UK, Canada or US) and simply waiting for the post, to arrive, with all the attendant registration forms, and other paraphernalia associated with the particular Professional Body, with which you hoped one day, to become part of, hopefully for the rest of your life.

Thereafter, it meant getting down to the grindstone of "after hours studying", until it was time to sit the first tranche of exams for say, the Foundation Certificate stage, through to the advanced Professional Finals, some 12-14 plus subjects later.

Today I recognize that all of the short listing process and eventual registration with a UK Distance ED College in preparation for undertaking the first foundation courses was by all accounts, a miracle in its own right, so thanks be to God.

'The fear of the Lord is the beginning of wisdom, and knowledge of the Holy one, is understanding' (Proverbs 9;10)

CHAPTER SIX (6)

Who Did You Talk To Out There—(College Days)

A few years later, now at full time College in the UK, it was at Statistics class one day, dealing with "Law of Probability" and related statistical techniques, that my learned Professor was seeking to outline to the group of students who made up my class, the merits (and demerits) of the use of Statistical formula, in the Management of Business.

This was quite "early days" in the course and I suspect, sounded more like a "foreign language" to the uninitiated student body that we were, at that stage of the semester.

Wonderful stuff (after you have digested it) but not before—"Calculate the Coefficient of Rank Correlation'; 'Consider the Bi variate and multi variate situations of'; Estimate the "population regression equation",

"Design an Operations Research model using mathematical techniques in quantifying Management problems"—Ok you get the drift . . . .

It all sounded like 'double - Dutch' to me at the time and so I spontaneously shot to my feet and exited the class, going perhaps unknowingly for a "campus walk about ", and to what I thought, would help "clear my head" of the proverbial 'cobwebs'!!

As I walked the never ending tiled corridors of the Business Administration faculty, I went past a gents wash room and decided to pay a visit.

As I washed my hands and looked at myself in the mirror, I could not help but observe the grimace on my face and the aura of perplexity, resulting therefrom.

I have just got to get this subject under my belt, come "hell or high water"!

"Let's make our enemies our foot stools" came some biblical thoughts.

I clasped my hands onto both sides of the face basin, and offered up a prayer asking the Almighty to "open up my mind to the new concepts now before me" and I vowed that I would master the subjects over the coming weekend, when I sit to do my "clinical reviews", alone in my room.

That having been decided, I then ambled back to the classroom, by which time some half hour plus had elapsed and the professor was by then on the 'OHP' (Over head projector), asking the class to respond to the sequence required, in answer to the sample question he had presented.

Deciding I was a "non starter" at this stage, I sought to 'ignore' his requests for answers, but out of the 'corner' of my eye, I still found myself looking up at the Projector Screen.

With deafening silence in the room, I suddenly blurted out, "Would it be so and so sir?" "Yes that's correct," came Dr. Paynes reply.

And having done so, what do you think should happen next?

Again another period of deafening silence.

"Should it be so and so sir?" I again hesitatingly breathed out a response . . . Say that again Malcolm?

"That's exactly correct—Who did you talk to out there?"

"Nobody Sir," was my "feeble reply".

The class then erupted with "Oh these foreigners"!!

He must have gone out there and consulted his "ju-ju-Beans" . . . these (black) guys know something called 'voodoo' . . . or some such allegation.

No idea as to what that was all about, as I too had not even realized up to then, that I had apparently grasped the Statistical Concept, having missed over half of the tuition class.

That evening, I went by the college library to see whether I could find any past exam papers on the subject.

Went back to my room and began to attempt 2 or 3 past exam questions on the related subject, and put my answers aside to take them to my Course Professor for assessment, the following day.

About a week later, his assessment results came back at 92%, in what he described as "distinction level"!

What? How did this happen? From a position where I was becoming a candidate for an imminent "nervous breakdown", to "distinction level"??

The answer even for years eluded me, but today has now become clear—it was certainly not my strength, certainly not mine alone.

"Prayer changes everything". As it says in Matthew Ch17;v20 'Nothing shall be impossible to them that believe'.

I can still recall the layout of the gents washroom where the "miracle" occurred.

I remembered then and still do, the promise, "Ask and you shall receive, seek and you shall find, knock and it shall be opened unto you." Matthew Ch7; v7.

My People, all praise to the most high God.

CHAPTER SEVEN (7)

The Racial Divide—
(Real Or Imagined)

As a young St.Lucian working with a British based Company during the pre-Independence era, one soon had to learn 'ones place' in the scheme of things, so when ones College professors start to question, what are you doing over here(in UK) and why are you (even bothering) studying Business Management?

What is it you intend to manage, often with a tone so "cynical", that you may perhaps begin to doubt even your own long term goals, aspirations & ambitions?

That 'cloudy' setting was once created by a one time lecturer in Business Communications in imparting his expertise to my Class on comparative methods for communication in business and the cost, modes, channels and models of communication, the statistical reduction of the 'Arc of Distortion' through analysis of what the sender "actually transmits" as distinct from what the sender "intended to transmit", in order to achieve full understanding, between the communicating parties.

Ok, let me spare you the painful details, but by now again, you have caught my drift.

However, when Mr. Professor got on to the subject of Telecommunications Equipment, that was a different story because, believe it or not, working for the local Telecoms Company was back then my first choice for a job, but as they were requiring me to leave home for studies overseas within weeks of signing on, I opted instead for placement in the "shipping" field, and ultimately joined the then 'Geest Organisation'.

Anyway, a question was posed by Mr. Lecturer on what the class considered (wait for it) "the advantage of telex over telephones." (takes you back a bit eh?)

That's an "easy one"—answers began to spout from all corners of the class, but when I ventured to indicate the feature I had by then come to know about, being the pre programming of telex messages which could be "rattled" through in seconds thereafter, I was suddenly faced, with the lecturers retort, "hello, hello", he said 'I thought you people were into carrier pigeons.'

Many a statement like this, had led to student outbursts and even 'riots' at Universities, especially those with a sizable 'afro' student population, but I decided to ignore it and instead just 'took a deep breath'!

Being human, I must admit, that some 'choice words' did cross my mind, but instead these were replaced with the Psalm, "Though I walk through the valley of the shadow of death, I will fear no evil, for thou art with me"—

Praise be to the Lord . . . . I went on to finish my course . . . . I did not erupt!

CHAPTER EIGHT (8)

'Houses You Did Not Build'

I t all started with the acquisition of a "surplus" glass sliding door purchased off a building site at Massacre Hill in Roseau

St.Lucia, when at the age of 19, I somehow decided that it was time to start acquiring components for what might ultimately become my own house, based again on a "family" mandate, that as soon as we siblings could, we should "get our own keys"!

As the eldest of my siblings, every opportunity thereafter, I would see myself "analyzing" the Inventory of Hardware stores looking for "deals" which once located, I would enter into "terms" with the proprietors to purchase, and to which any "windfall" would be quickly applied.

In time, I had accumulated light fixtures, sanitary ware, metal windows, corrugated galvanize sheets, nails, screws, nuts & bolts, you name it, and even began sourcing furniture and household inventory, but still, I had no house!

My Mom (bless her) jokingly shared with her friends, that "this boy must be crazy" as unlike the other boys who would perhaps bring home a "girl friend" (or two), he keeps bringing in doors, windows and other hardware stuff. (lol)

Having utilized all storage areas at the family home, overflows were later carried over to my uncle's house higher up the road and ultimately, a small store room in a rented apartment on the Morne.

In the interim, I was able to acquire a residential plot and to service this debt, took on a couple extra jobs working in an Hotel after hours, and "dabbling" in Insurance Sales on weekends.

The age of 21-22, saw the commencement of the construction of what would ultimately become my very first home, which on completion, I occupied for an initial period, before leasing it out and leaving home to go complete my studies overseas.

Looking back over the years, I believe that it was the "spark of faith" with the purchase of that first "sliding door", which made that house project come to fruition, so early in my adult life.

These are not coincidences, but can all be put down to the goodness of God, and the faith we place in him and which it is essential that we recognize, as he begins to put opportunities in our path.

If we can do this, God is going to continue to open "supernatural doors" for us and to remove all impediments to the achievement of our aspirations.

My late Godfather once said to me, never be afraid to tackle "big things", as they were only a number of "small things" strung together!

So I can only deduce that the "faith" demonstrated by acquiring the first sliding door, followed by windows, light fixtures etc, long before I had even a house lot to my name, was the beginning of that supernatural outcome, which I have since tried replicating several times in various forms, in the course of my life.

Even to this day, I am never quite sure 'where the money will come from' for what I intend to do, but where there is a will, there is way every time.

To those who dare to believe, I again quote Psalms 9:10 which says "Those who know your name will trust in you, for you Lord, have never forsaken those who seek you."

To God be the glory.

CHAPTER NINE (9)

For A Daughter

To my two daughters (H&H) the following poetic lines were penned in 1996 and published via The CARICOM (Caribbean Community) Secretariat in 2004, speaks to the benevolent intervention of the Almighty, in guiding their paths to this day.

Notwithstanding the challenges faced during their early upbringing, their personal and professional accomplishments to date, are testimony to God's unconditional goodness and protection that he accords us, as articulated in Psalms 23 V4 which says'Though I walk through the valley of the shadow of death, I will fear no evil, for thou art with me'.

So to my two daughters, I humbly dedicate this poem;—

'FOR A DAUGHTER'

With joy unbounded
She came into our world,
Full of hope and expectation,
Love, unconditional love,

She walked, she bloomed,
She blossomed into pre-adolesence,
I recall the plaided outfit,
That was her school uniform

Then she grew up,
Sight unseen, except
The occasional exchange,
Via a remote mechanism,
To avoid further acrimony,

Despite all this, yet
She persevered,
Through thick and thin,
Through joy and pain,
To reach the goal post,
Of her early ambitions,
May the Almighty grant her Peace.

(Ends-1996)

For those of us going through what feels like 'the valley of the shadow of death", even those tough times we are all facing in some form or other today, when we feel down and out, discouraged and frustrated, I commend to you the Biblical reminder shared by one of my favourite international Pastors (Lakewoods Joel Osteen) of the Almightys assurance, that he is walking beside you, strengthening you and making a way where there seems to be no way.

Yes, we are just "walking thought the valley" and the challenges we are facing, are to be considered as only temporary.

All praise to the most high God for walking beside us, even in the toughest times of our lives and seeing us through safely to the other side of whatever the circumstances we may be facing.

The Book of Isaiah Ch 41;10 says "Fear thou not, for I am with thee; be not dismayed for I am thy God; I will uphold thee with the right hand of my righteousness"

May God continue to bless them, as they make their own way through the challenges as are defined by the world in which we live today . . .

Gods Blessings and praise to the most high . . .

CHAPTER TEN (10)

'Corporate Governance'

U ltimately breaking through the glass ceiling from' office junior' to Corporate Governance & Senior Management responsibility level, at first seemed quite elusive, but as years rolled by, it became a way of life as I got quite busy just doing the job entrusted to me and doing it to the best of my ability.

The momentum after some years of intensity and perhaps even' frustration 'on occasions, prompted the following poetic lines which I dedicated back then to those aspiring towards careers in 'Business Administration".

The reflection was especially true as time drew closer to my planned "early" retirement, back in the early 1990's.

The Poem all went something like this and which my 'old' University ventured to Publish in their alumni magazine and which I too included in one of my own Poetry Book publications titled '55 Sensations' . . . so here goes . . .

Call "Administration"

If the roof should spring a leak
Call Administration
Or when stationery stocks you seek
Call Administration
When the're meetings to arrange

Or the a/c behaves strange
When you feel its time for change
Call Administration

If the're telephones to install
Call Administration
To replace hangings on the wall
Call Administration
When the're lawyers that prevail
On that account that's doomed to fail
Then with one accord we hail
Call Administration

When the're visitors from abroad
Call Administration
To see the plant or meet the Board
Call Administration
When their contracts to be signed
Precisely on the dotted line
Whether its buildings, cars or jeeps
Insurance policies that are for keeps
Call Administration

When there's need to advertise
Call Administration
From "press release" to "give a prize"
Call Administration
When you find the goods inventory

To modify is elementary
To pleasure peasantry or gentry
Call Administration

When you need a new recruit
Call Administration
Or when there's need to "give the boot"
Call Administration
And when in sickness you lament
That medical cover was you intent
Rest assured you'll not relent
Call Administration

* * * * * * * * * * * * * *

Praise & Honour to the Almighty for having successfully served an initial 25 year sojourn in the field of Business Administration, which I continue to this day in a more Consultancy capacity, 40 years plus later.

CHAPTER ELEVEN (11)

'Ebenezer House' where I grew up

Humanitarianism—
"The Ultimate Joy"

It was the late Paul Percy Harris, born in Wisconsin USA on 19th April 1868, who graduated in 1891, later became the Founder of the world's largest Humanitarian Organization, known today as Rotary International, who, in his quest to encourage the important upholding of high ethical standards in business and professions, revealed that "Rotary Clubs had an obligation to carry out Vocational (& Community) service projects designed to increase employment opportunities in the community, promote a fair work place environment and raise awareness and appreciation of all useful occupations."

That charge to my mind, speaks to the Biblical assurance, that "In as much as you have done it unto one of the least of thy brethren, you have done it unto me." Matthew Ch25; v40.

In that regard, I was "energized" when I received the provisional support of my siblings residing both locally and overseas, that we would facilitate the availability of former Charles (Ebenezer) family home (vested in us by our parents the late Percy and Alvina Charles) for conversion into a Humanitarian Centre, to be operated under the joint aegis of

The Rotary Club of St. Lucia and other kindred agencies.

"The Rotary House" as it would be possibly renamed (from "Ebenezer house") would provide access to the following services inter alia:—

a) Youth Counseling and Skills Training
b) Wheel Chair Distribution
c) Citizens Advisory Bureau
d) Spiritual and Ethical Guidance
e) Music Lessons to Disadvantaged Youth
f) Linkages with the Rotary Mobile Counseling Unit

Collaboration with the National Skills Development Centre, the James Belgrave Micro Enterprise Fund (Belfund), The Planned Parenthood Association, RISE, The Inter Church Council and The Ministry of Social Transformation would be enlisted to provide relevant programmes, to create hope for the future for disadvantaged young persons and their life aspirations.

While my own aspirations for a successful outcome of the project are sometimes clouded by concerns over the unavailability of adequate funding and manpower, I am encouraged by the words of the Bible Book of Matthew 21v 21 (NKV) which says, "Jesus answered and said unto them, Verily I say unto you, If ye have faith, and doubt not, ye shall not only do this which is done to the fig tree, but also if ye shall say to the mountain be thou removed and be thou cast into the sea, it shall be done."

The "mountain" we face in assembling all of the pieces which would make our aspirations possible, will be removed, as I was taught by faith, that instead of speaking about how "big the challenges are," we should instead, speak to the challenges, about how "big our God is."!

Therefore when we release our faith in this manner, God often shows up himself and removes whatever impediments that may be present in our paths.

Almighty God, I thank you in advance for the favour you will grant as I speak to the challenges (mountains) standing in my path, in Jesus' name.Amen.

Notwithstanding the persistent prevailing economic recession and all of its attended manmade wars, I look forward with faith to the (Rotary Ebenezer House) Humanitarian Centre, becoming a reality one day, by God's grace.

CHAPTER TWELVE (12)

'New Found Love'

I got back home in late 1980 from UK studies and decided to visit my "roots" by attending my local Church Sunday School Picnic, one public holiday.

All the while trying to mind my own business, I was suddenly "hit for six" by a stunning young lass, whom I thought at the time was far too young, but whom I ultimately married (following lots of global "research") and in whose honour the following Poetic lines were penned in the 1990's titled namely:—

'SELMALC'

(1)

There was once a young lady
With charms so immense
That caused a young man to 'lose all his sense'
He thought it befitting to make her his bride
In good and in bad times, he'd be at her side

(2)

As the years rolled along
They matured well together
That friends looking on, called them
'Birds of a feather'
Come business or pleasure
They made several plans
To master at home
And in faraway lands

(3)

One by one, all the while
Dreams began to unfold
That the final results
Were a sight to behold
The business that started
With a number of two
Soon grew in its stature
To hold you know who
The long hours paid off
It was all plain to see
Notwithstanding constraints of
E-C-O-N-O-M-Y

(4)

And now in conclusion
Let us give thanks to God
For what started off as
'Two peas in a pod'
The two had become just inseparable
Like the wings of a bird or what else we label
No doubt on reflection
They always meant well
Despite those who often
Tried to give them some h—

(5)

Let us all then encourage
Those things that are good
And try most vehement
For the heights that we could
And time in its passing
We should never relent
To help those with passion
For the best of intent.

(Ends)

Now need I say more . . . ?

Except to thank God for helping me find a life-long partner, who was (and I consider still is) compatible with my own personality and long term aspirations.

CHAPTER THIRTEEN (13)

'Divine Health
Interventions'

a) <u>Cardio Challenge</u>

It was about 5:20 p.m. that I sat in my private business office, putting together what was to be a collective response by the local Private Sector to a proposed Governmental introduction of new labour legislation, intended to manage the Nations Human Resources.

With fairness and equity in mind, the then Private Sector Council of Saint Lucia, consisting of Presidents who had met the day before and tabled comments, suggestions & concerns emanating from their respective sub sectors, whether they be from a Hospitality Industry perspective, a Commerce perspective, a Manufacturing perspective, Small Medium Entrepreneurs, Micro Enterprise Vendors and the associated Informal Sector, all perspectives were to be taken on board.

Faced with a pressing deadline, I was perhaps "fast forwarding" myself to complete the collation process and to submit our "master" response to the Governmental Authorities in the shortest time possible.

All of a sudden, the room began to "get darker and darker and darker." Were we experiencing a power failure?

No, my hypertensive blood pressure had apparently exceeded its limits and I was coming down with a "cardiac attack", resulting in my ultimate collapse into a semi-conscious state.

About that same time,'something' seemed to prompt my wife to spontaneously unlock the general office door and come to my office 'cubicle' saying something to the effect, "can you sign a cheque for "xyz", as we need it first thing tomorrow morning."

When she noticed according to her account I had "turned purple", she realized that something was gravely wrong and began to summon an Ambulance, to take me to the Hospital Emergency.

She apparently encountered some difficulties in getting the urgent response from The Ambulance Service she was looking for and so a "plan B" was quickly put into action, by asking one of the staff to bring her car round to the back of the office building, and with help from security guards, I was carried out onto the back seat of her car, and sped away to the Hospital Emergency Room for Medical intervention.

My personal Doctor was alerted by phone en route to the Hospital and once the Emergency Staff had done their best to "stabilize" me overnight, I was relocated the following day to the wards, for continued assessment and monitoring.

Three days plus into my Hospital stay, I recall my Doctor saying words to my wife to the effect "You got him here right on time, otherwise . . . ."

Now fully recovered from what was diagnosed back then as a "mild heart attack", I can only credit "divine intervention" for causing my wife and Business partner to return to a locked up office, to have me sign a cheque (which I suspect might have easily been signed the following day).

What prompted her to visit my office at that time, when all staff had already been done for the day?

The scripture says "In all your ways acknowledge him and he shall direct your paths" (Proverbs 3:6 NKJ)

I am still here today, and I know fully well who was responsible for working that outcome through my wife, so let me humbly proclaim yet again, "to God be the Glory."

b) <u>The Big "C"—(Men take note)</u>

When your "PSA" (Prostate Specific Antigen) suddenly "spikes" way past its customary readings, it becomes or should become, cause for concern.

That was the experience I had back in 2004, when I went in for my routine annual (head to toe) physicals.

I didn't feel any pain and all seemed quite normal, but no, there was the Big "C" creeping into my system, with the "stealth of a nuclear bomber".

No I don't believe it,—lets do the test again I said . . . and again . . .

But it was for real . . . the results were consistent, the time had come like a "thief in the night".

As one who had consistently kept a diary for all of his career life, I suddenly found myself simply reluctant to write down any of my appointments, especially the "long term" ones, due some months away, like a Conference, business travel, or even an impending visit by a relative or friend.

No, I had even began to lose the' psychological will' if you like, to press on with my goals and found myself preparing mentally, for what I thought, may be my imminent exit, from "this world into the next."

Yes, I had faith, yes I know that God had always come through for me in the past, but was this it?

My faith was being tested . . . no doubt about it so I thought . . .

I know "one out of one" has to die, so then, had "my number" now come up?

On quiet reflection, I again recalled the passage of the scripture which says, in the Book of Psalms #23 "Though I walk through the valley of the shadow of death, I will fear no evil, for thou art with me."

Had learned and recited this several times since I was a kid, but was I now being called upon to put my faith to the test?

The Secretary at the office of my Urologist called with my next appointment date.

The curative options, each with its attendant "side effects" having been spelt out to me, I eventually selected one that I would have to "live with", if I acted quickly, before the cancer began to invade the "non retractable" parts of my anatomy.

The words of one of my favorite televangelists also came to mind (from the Pastoral telecasts of Joel Osteen) "No matter what you are facing today, know this—you are not alone". Don't allow fear to paralyze you in the middle of "the valley of the shadow of death—remember God is with you, he is walking beside you and is making a way of escape for you".

Powerful words, which call for true faith to believe in, especially when one was at his lowest ever level of self confidence.

He continues "you will be brought out of that tight place, into a place of strength and victory—so don't give up—start to get a vision of your life, on the other side of your problem."

Dear readers, by God's grace, and the skills of my physicians both at home and overseas, I am today "Cancer free' and doing my best to encourage other men, to take their cancer tests on a regular (annual) basis, and my dear ladies, the same applies to you.

Let us use our God given intelligence, to help save each other lives.

Without hesitation . . . To God be the glory.

CHAPTER FOURTEEN (14)

Rotary International Emblem-
Have been a member 30 plus years

'Responding to the "Clarion Call" to Service'

I am still a believer that "if something works for you, don't try to fix it," ...

Now in my sixties, I believe I have truly found my rightful niche in life, based again on the premise, that, "In as much as you have done it to one the least of your brethren, you have done it unto me".

My interest in humanitarian matters, as indeed my interest in Corporations, started when I was just a kid.

I recall building a replica of the city of Castries, under the avocado tree in my parent's backyard, complete with Street Lights, Shops, Printery, Cinema, School, Fire Station and the like, which my younger brothers and myself took charge of, with an ever increasing passion.

Powered by a "mega" battery we had purchased downtown, we lit up the city each night (before Dad would call a halt, in favour of our homework).

We were proud of our little "city" with (toy) Cars, Vans and Trucks parked outside each of the Business houses and began to see ourselves as "City managers", even though "miles away" from any such exposure, except that our "Uncle Ju" was on the Mayoral trail of that era.

It was a little project that we loved dearly until one day, it was considered that it was an unbalanced encroachment on our "real world" school work, and was summarily relegated to the nearest garbage disposal bin.!!

That none the less, did not deter my own thoughts of being a business person of some sort one day, even if the path to such a career, was still very unclear.

By 1966, my Dad had joined "something" which he called "Rotary" which was, as I understood it back then, an organisation for business men, who wanted to "give something back" to their community.

I was at St. Mary's College high school by then and from time to time, went with him on projects, where I assisted in setting up the tents, loading the vans with Charity stuff and witnessed the enthusiasm of these "business persons" manifesting itself, in ways I had never imagined.

Were they being paid for such work and if so, how could I qualify?

Still some 3-4 years away from even getting my first entry level job was possible, these "grown up guys", were "giving back" to help those in need.

Having left high school and gotten my first job, the next 10-12 years would see me gradually moving through the ranks and at the same time, studying "Distance Ed" and full time in the UK,(as alluded to in my earlier chapters) towards the pinnacle of my chosen Business Management career.

Upon my UK college graduation and return home to take up an appointment "at Board Level", I was one day approached by a couple Senior Rotarians, one of whom worked as an Auditor, in a firm which handled my then Company's Accounts.

They invited me to "come as their guest" to a Rotary meeting one Friday on their lunch hour.

The name "Rotary" was quite familiar, having been exposed to it way back in "high school", as alluded to earlier.

I went along once, twice, three times maybe, when they asked whether I would consider "induction" into the Club.

It all seemed to sit well at the time with my work schedule and fuelled by my inner desire to become "Your brother's keeper", as I had learned early since my Sunday School days.

The rest as they say "is history", as some thirty (30) plus years on, I am still an avid participant in the humanitarian Programs of Rotary, which I envisage, as a practical application of the "Biblical" principles, of caring for your fellow man—"Your brother's keeper".

For my "sins", I was quickly appointed Club Secretary for two consecutive terms, Club Director 3 or 4 times in various "Avenues of Service" (as the specializations of Rotary are called) Vice President, Club President, and later Assistant District Governor and even

District Governor Nominee, latter of which, I had no choice but to demit, when the ravages of Hurricane Tomas devastated the infrastructure of my homeland, which had already been grappling internally with the impact of global recession.

That having been said, what to my mind was most important, was the "Your brother's keeper" component, which manifested itself through local community projects, including constructing laundry shower units for Bilharzia Eradication, Donations of School books, Scholarships, Wheel chairs, Medical assistance to disadvantaged persons, Mobile blood Banks, Hurricane & Disaster Relief, and the list goes on.

Internationally to date, Rotary club members worldwide have also contributed more than US$1 billion toward the eradication of polio, a cause Rotary took on in 1985, and which the World Health Organization, UNICEF, U.S. Centers for Disease Control and Prevention, all joined with Rotary, as spearheading partners of the Global Polio Eradication Initiative.

The Bill Gates Foundation since then, become a major supporter and in 2007, gave Rotary a $100 million challenge grant for polio eradication, increasing it to $355 million by 2009 and Rotary agreed to raise $200 million in matching funds by June 30, 2012.

I therefore pay tribute to one of the "dominant" organizations that has come to be major part of my life for well over 30 years, and one to which I had penned some poetic lines, later converted into Rotary Saint Lucia's modest contribution to the Centenial of Rotary, performed on stage at world International Convention in Chicago, USA in 2005, by the Rotary Calabashers Group, and of which the author has had the honour to be the Groups' Founder, and which 'storytelling' lyrics went like this . . . .

CHAPTER FIFTEEN (15)

"Service Above Self"— 100 Years

(1)

From a concept that started in 1905
Grew a culture devoted to keep good alive
Dedication that swept through
a room of just four
Was the key to the project
that opened the door
To a great humane friendship and charity
That today is known worldwide
as R-O-T-A-R-Y

(2)

As the concept of sharing grew far and wide
Appealing to thousands to help stem the tide
Of ill health, disability and poverty too
On a scale to the world, was entirely new
To foster goodwill, understanding and peace
The collective effort had begun to increase

(3)

Today, as our numbers have risen to millions
Notwithstanding periodic detracting opinions
From country to country it's
clear we accomplish
Assistance where needed to
those lost and impoverish
The council on legislation
has since thought if fit
To extend Rotary's work to the youth just a bit

(4)

So Rotaract and Interact were recently born
To a world where youths often
are held in some scorn
Their involvement in full "Service above Self"
Will open the way to their
growth and good health

So let us pay tribute to a
great man Paul Harris
Whether based in St.Lucia, Barbados or Paris
For a highway that leads us to a greater good
To those in our country, for
whose caring we should

(5)

And now as we celebrate 100 years
A reason to relegate all foregone fears
Of doubt and uncertainty, to name just a few
As we harness our strengths
and our sinues renew
The successful ambitions of our founders four
The fire, that stirred, across nations galore
Our destiny beckons, continue even still
That Four-Way Test, to all men of goodwill

By Malcolm A.J.Charles
The Rotary Club of St.Lucia-2004 (D-7030)

Again, I am indeed honored and humbled at the distinction of being the composer of these lines that led to the establishment of the "Rotary Calabashers" Group, which continues to produce Benefit Concerts for Charitable causes across Saint Lucia to this day.

All Praise, thanks and Glory to the most high . . . .

"The Rotary Calabashers' performing Group,who raise funds annually for Charitable causes in Saint Lucia."

CHAPTER SIXTEEN (16)

On Becoming Debt Free—"The Miracle"

With God all things are possible . . .

So go "Sow a seed in time of need". If you want God to solve your problem, go and help someone else with theirs, as it says in Isaiah 38, "Trust in the Lord and Do Good" (to somebody else).

Whoever would have thought, that from the "trenches" of business (and personal) Debt, compounded by a stubborn global recession, that we would arise from those ashes, to the "declaration", that we were now "Totally Debt Free"?

Let me quickly share that I speak here in futuristic "tongues," as my present circumstances are anything but . . . (so by faith, my future text is to be written)

Isaiah continues 'They that wait upon the Lord shall renew their strength, they shall mount up with wings like eagles, they shall run and not be weary, they shall walk and not faint . . . (to be continued as I offer thanks to the Almighty in advance.)

CHAPTER SEVENTEEN (17)

Epilogue

S hould one write his own "obituary"??

I should think not, even though I suppose there may be instances where this may very well happen.

It was at the induction service of a new Superintendent Minister of St.Lucia Methodist Church (Rev Madet Merove) that I was invited back in 2011, to render a musical tribute.

Backed up by the Church Youth Choir (under its meticulous Music Director with whom I had rehearsed on a couple occasions), we were set to stage a now popular Gospel rendition of a song titled "You Raise Me Up", with myself as lead singer and at which event I was honoured to perform for more reasons that one . . . I just love singing Gospel as I believe I disclosed earlier in my 'manuscript' . . .

I had also been asked by the Church steward, to let them have "some notes" on my (musical) background, which I penned out of what I could recall from a church/ charity perspective.

Somehow having summarized the requested notes, I began to feel like I was 'writing my own obituary', as opposed to an introduction of a "feature singer".

It read in a way which now I can only dedicate to the Church that with my parents early insistence, gave me a start in life and from which today, I still continue to draw spiritual encouragement and sustainance . . .

"Son of a former Methodist Sunday School Superintendent, Choir Tenor and Methodist Infant School Principal, the late Percy and Alvina Charles, Malcolm Charles literally "grew up" within the walls of the St. Lucia Methodist Church, being exposed to its teachings, gaining both a spiritual and academic foundation, while performing with his family Gospel group at home called "The Ebenezer Quartet", comprising his two brothers, his sister and himself.

Apart from membership of the Methodist Youth Fellowship, he sang in the Sunday School Choir, the Church Choir and in 1969, became a Founding Member of the 'Yuletide Choral Group', which focused on charitable performances at homes for the Elderly, Hospitals, Prisons and other related Institutions.

He also had a brief stint as a Singer and Organist in the "public entertainment domain", with both the "N-DEES Combo" and then "The Quavers Orchestra".

Following his return home from Business Studies in the UK, he joined the Rotary Club of Saint Lucia and for the next two decades, took the lead in a number of major charitable projects (including St.Lucia's first Rotary Mobile Blood Bank) which project is said to have saved the lives of thousands of persons islandwide each year.

In 2004, he founded a new charitable music performing group currently known as "The Rotary Calabashers" who performed his signature composition titled "Service above Self—100 years" as a tribute to Rotary International's Centenial, live on stage at the Chicago Convention Centre USA in June 2005, for which standing ovations were given by a circa 5,000 plus member audience.

The "Rotary Calabashers Group" continues in their long standing tradition of staging Benefit Concerts annually for worthy charitable causes in Saint Lucia, with projects worth several thousand dollars being contributed to the disadvantaged in our community.

Malcolm Charles as Founder of "The Calabashers" and their former Chair, holds membership of the US based International Fellowship of Rotarian Musicians.

He enjoys singing and playing Gospel and Folk music with keyboards and Guitar during his spare time and continues to rehearse and perform on stage with the Group.

Today, he returns to his home base church with one of his favourite gospel pieces titled "You Raise Me Up" backed up by theMethodist Youth Choir, under the baton of Mrs. Deanna Clarke, Musical Director.

While the notes look like and seem to say what I believe they ought to say, somehow I sense this "nagging" feeling, that I was penning my own obituary . . . . hopefully I am wrong . . . at least not quite yet.

But just in case there may be any truth to it, let me take early o'clock take the opportunity to thank the Methodist Church and all of its institutions for the "foundation" given to me and my siblings from childhood to the present day.

Talking about childhood, you know there was a time back then that I even wanted to become a practicing Methodist Minister and use to emulate the Church Ministers, by placing my mothers bed sheets or table cloths or whatever, over my back, and "preaching" to passers by from my childhood home veranda at Mongiraud in Castries . . . .

That was close but strange enough, I escaped "that net", but never lost my appreciation of the "showers of blessings" I have had fall on my life ever since then, despite the many challenges faced in between and which I still continue to face.

I still have plans one day to preach a 'real sermon' somewhere . . . its never too late and so the 'My Testimony' booklet could be a step in that very direction . . . you never know . . .

So meanwhile, let never forget to give thanks for the 'Showers of Blessing' we continue to receive along lifes journey here on earth.

As the songwriter says and I quote:—

There shall be showers of blessing;
This is the promise of love
There shall be seasons refreshing
Sent from the saviour above.

Chorus

Showers of blessing,
Showers of blessing we need
Mercy drops round us are falling,
But for the showers we plead.

There shall be showers of blessing,
Precious reviving again;
Over the hills and the valleys,
Sound of abundance of rain.

There shall be showers of blessing,
Send them upon us, O Lord
Grant to us now a refreshing;
Come, and now honour Thy World.

There shall be showers of blessing,
Oh, that today they might fall
Now, as to God we're confessing
Now, as on Jesus we call.

There shall be showers of blessing,
If we but trust and obey
There shall be seasons refreshing
If we let God have his way.

Arising from those promised "showers of blessing", I repeat as in my poetry lines, that the scriptures assure us in (John 10:10), if we can keep our faith that "I came that you might have life and have it more abundantly".

No matter what is going on in our lives, we were meant to "live life to the full" (abundantly) and to receive the fullest blessings of our God.

Yes, give it a try . . . . and I offer up my humble praise to the most high God, in accordance with the mandate of Psalm 34:1 which says "I will bless the Lord at all times, his praise shall continually be in my mouth."

I believe God has a good plan for all of us, if only we would let him.

Ends.